MR AND MRS SCOTLAND ARE DEAD

By Kathleen Jamie

POETRY

Black Spiders (Salamander Press, 1982)
A Flame in Your Heart, with Andrew Greig (Bloodaxe Books, 1986)
The Way We Live (Bloodaxe Books, 1987)
The Autonomous Region: poems & photographs from Tibet
   with Sean Mayne Smith (Bloodaxe Books, 1993)
The Queen of Sheba (Bloodaxe Books, 1994)
Jizzen (Picador, 1999)
Mrs and Mrs Scotland Are Dead: Poems 1980-1994
   (Bloodaxe Books, 2002)

RECORDING

The Poetry Quartets: 1 (British Council / Bloodaxe Books, 1998)
   [with Simon Armitage, Jackie Kay & Glyn Maxwell]

TRAVEL

The Golden Peak (Virago, 1992)

Kathleen Jamie

MR AND MRS SCOTLAND ARE DEAD

ARE DEAD

POEMS 1980-1994

SELECTED BY LILIAS FRASER

BLOODAXE BOOKS

ISBN: 1 85224 586 7

First published 2002 by
Bloodaxe Books Ltd,
Highgreen,
Tarset,
Northumberland NE48 1RP.

www.bloodaxebooks.com
For further information about Bloodaxe titles
please visit our website or write to
the above address for a catalogue.

Bloodaxe Books Ltd acknowledges
the financial assistance of Northern Arts.

Cover printing by J. Thomson Colour Printers Ltd, Glasgow.

Printed in Great Britain by
Cromwell Press Ltd, Trowbridge, Wiltshire.

Acknowledgements

This book reprints poems from Kathleen Jamie's first five collections, *Black Spiders* (Salamander Press, 1982), *A Flame in Your Heart* (Bloodaxe Books, 1986), *The Way We Live* (Bloodaxe Books, 1987), *The Autonomous Region* (Bloodaxe Books, 1993) and *The Queen of Sheba* (Bloodaxe Books, 1994). Four poems from *Black Spiders* were reprinted in *The Way We Live* but are here included in the original collection. *A Flame in Your Heart* was a collaboration with poet Andrew Greig, broadcast by BBC Radio 4 in a shortened version under the title *Rumours of Guns* in 1985; the epigraph is from a song by Marcue, Benjemin, Durham and Seiler. *The Autonomous Region* was a collaboration of poems and photographs from Tibet with Sean Mayne Smith.

This selection has been made by Lilias Fraser. It includes two previously uncollected poems, 'View from the Cliffs', first published in *Aquarius*, and 'Dreaming of Espionage', first published in *Blind Serpent*.

Contents

The Queen of Sheba (1994)

View from the Cliffs

Orkney rises like the letter D,
gently rolls,
then
nothing, save the ocean
and twenty thousand seabirds
stirring a storm in a teapot.

Between the rocks a walnut lifts
lobsters for London.
Philosophical fishermen, content
in their wisdom – The answer?
A walking-pace world.

[1979]

FROM

BLACK SPIDERS

(1982)

Black Spiders

He looked up to the convent
she'd gone to. She answered no questions
but he knew by the way she'd turned away
that morning.
He felt like swimming to the caves.

*

The nuns have retreated. The eldest still
peals the bell in glee, although no one comes
from the ruins. All their praying was done
when they first saw the ships and the Turks'
swords reflecting the sun.

In the convent the cistern is dry,
the collection boxes empty – cleft skulls
severed and bleached,
are kept in a shrine, and stare to the East.

*

She caught sight of him later, below, brushing salt
from the hair of his nipples. She wanted them
to tickle; black spiders on her lips.

Women in Jerusalem

'Alo! Germanee? Welcome! Alo! America?'
I hid from the spat crudities of Arabs,
the continuous stare, unblinking sun,
in a crumbling dorm all hanging with garments.
A drowsy voice asked 'Alo, Englis?'
We were instantly friends.

In the market we discussed wares
in gobbledegook for the sake of peace.
We talked, in the shade of the hostel,
of the world's brute men, money, politics
and the good things of home.

On the balcony we sat above the flies,
the broad mules' backs, brown Bedouin hands
weighing and arguing figs; she spat
an insect from her fingers, handed money
to her husband. I saw a man
at the Damascus Gate, and cursed.

Obscured now and then by women in abayehs,
shaped like barrels and walking as barrels
would, hooped with belts. I was sure.
My friend peeped out. I was purdah'd: the door
opened into his view. We conferred like Arab sisters.

'I'd invited him to Massada, and split.
We don't understand each other
at all. "I," he said, "protect you."
From whom? He shrugged "It's our mentality".
I went alone:

On the plain in the haze the road is laid down
like an almighty crucifixion. At the junction
a fat hand twists my wrist. He offers
200 shequel, kaffiyas, toy camels,
the sundry geegaws of his stall and
a lift to Jerusalem.

His son watches and learns, and lets
ecstatic flies crawl over a scab in his ear.
There is dust; a mirage of a bus, a
sign of life. I run...'

We'd been under siege all afternoon,
telling tales, occasionally checking
and ducking. Neighbouring roofs
were reconnoitred for routes.
He expected my pale bare flesh
to mark me out, and sat tight.
We gave in towards night.

In the room were foul and ancient abaheys,
we hooped them round and laughed at ourselves.
They blacked out the sound of our voices
and hid our bodies from sight.

Abir

There is the future Abir told me about
in the room where she showed me photographs
and served Turkish coffee.

She stared at the black grounds in my cup.
There was a slight smell of camphor. She
nodded and smiled. Apparently

I think too much, and will make journeys. Tomorrow
she'll make coffee, and curl her sisters' hair. She
asked me only the English for 'husband'.

This morning Abir will buy fruit in the market:
her cane chair creaks to itself in the heat. She'll
be home before the sun lies smashed on the streets.

The Barometer

Last year
Mother threw the barometer
the length of the corridor. This:
she has set her jaw. There's a chill
and the rustle of weeds. She's come in
from the garden, now she'll withdraw.

The maids are shivering. Outside
they're talking of snow. I say no
to a fire – it's an act of surrender.

I can see the bare fields from here
on the balcony. The nights
are growing longer. I know.
At least the harvest is gathered and safe.
– Every thanksgiving
I dance like a Romany. Indian summers;
I giggle and weep. Mother and me
go picnics in the blossoming...

My furs are laid out and waiting.
The maids keep tutting.
I catch myself biting
dead skin from my lips.
I have played with my gloves all day.

I ought just to jump
and meet Hades half way.

The Harbour

At the centre, red and dripping
are wreckers' lights. By night
they await the occasional drift, but gallop
away at the fall of day, frustrated
by sure navigation and calm.

The harbour could be anywhere.
In its wall are a window, a board and door;
the home of a hermit whose
nights and days are tidal,
his house being rhythmically drowned.

On the board are meticulous notes,
on the rising and settling of waves,
his service to fishers and curious tourists:
only the price of paper – like this –
is requested and paid.

The dock where vessels leave is walked
by a resentful temptress who shrieks
if she catches you staring away from her legs.
She says she finds hammers
better than lovers.

Back country is as yet unexplored. They say
the sky is the colour of bruise. The sun:
underground. Rocks glow like night-lights
with the strain of containing it.

The Leaving of an Island

Every taken chasing step
in the parting dark
from the old barred door
made a few stars fade.
There were always more.

Now wildlife hides.
First boys then men have whistled past.
Last night – birds called.

Down the clearing road
milestones are measured out in years
each reached with slow, now knowing paces
towards the pier.
There the ferry waits.

November

He can touch me with a look
as thoughtless as afternoon
and think as much of hindering me
as he would of sailing away.

In November, when the storms come
he drums his fingers on his books and turns
them into a fist that crashes. On the shore
where he insists we walk, he holds me like a man
at a deck-rail in a gale. I suspect his eyes
are open, red and gazing over my head
in the direction of abroad.

I am left to tell him in a voice that
seems as casual as his talk of travel:
I think as much of leaving
as of forcing him to stay.

Inhumation

No one knows if he opened his eyes,
acknowledged the dark,
felt around, found and drank
the mead provided, supposing
himself dead.

Storm in Istanbul

Beware the temper of the only god.
We asked only rain to smother the dust.

By three we'd kicked off the single grey sheet.
The patrol passed in the alley.

We took it for a torch, a search, we could not speak
above the roar, we opened a window
and heard the boots. Leaned out, tongues out
to taste the rain.

In the flash you could read the armoured car's plate.
The guard saw moving shapes, fired
shouts between the cracking of petrified cloud.
He laughed too loud when
he linked arms with his chum
('Thought you was a terrorist, didn'I?')
Their uniforms scraped.

You could have shot him from here,
some mother's gaunt son. Not even having
his big boots on could save him
from flinching when his almighty blue mosque
was lit from above.
He crouched below his bayonet. It gleamed
like the minarets jabbing the sky
that shuddered and roared in pain.

Beside the rancid heap where it eats a dog wept.
All the cats howled. It gave him
the creeps. He whispered through his teeth
to calm them. For him
someone began to play a pipe,
a few shaking voices sang. Light was coming...

From the towers came the wail of a failing old imam.

The faithful went to pray.
The heathen, we slept.

Cramond Island

Most who choose the causeway cross
for a handful of years
turning back before the tide
cuts them off. They take up books
behind these windbreakers
we weave around us.

Come and scratch your feet
on sharper, more explosive shells.
Draw your own blood
for a farther view,
a place to lay bare
among ruins.
The choice will return in time.

Back in the study
they stare to sea, and heal,
marking pages with salt and sand
shaken from windblown hair.

Permanent Cabaret

Our highwire artiste,
knowing nothing of fear, will take
sparkling risks fifty feet high.
Her costume, ladies, is iced with
hard diamonds.
While she mounts all those steps
our old friend the clown will stand
upside down in a shower of confetti
and chirp 'Love me!'

Their lamp is the last on camp to go out.
Coco reads Jung, sometimes aloud to
Estelle, if she's sewing on sequins.
More often she practises alone in the ring
for the day she enters permanent cabaret,
perhaps in Zurich. Coco cracks his knuckles,
thinking vaguely of children, or considers
repainting the outside of their van.

Half way across Estelle glitters like frost.
She has frozen. 'Remain professional.' She
draws breath through her teeth, wavers
her hand: 'Let Coco sense something for once!'
His red boots are edging towards her. He
coaxes, offers aid – his absurd umbrella.
The audience wonder: is it part of the show
this embarrassing wobbling,
this vain desperation to clutch?

Dreaming of Espionage

I have to fall
into that square of rushing grey,
canvas flapping about my thighs.
Finger the cord, steel
myself. But hasn't the engine note changed?
The plane pitches down...

turns into a train, and all
I must do is jump from the wagon.
My mate hugs me roughly, urges me
out. It'll be the most beautiful day,

alone beside the track. Birds twitter,
I pick up my pack, walk to the spires
past fields of black earth (alive! alive!)

But there is more to this township
than business and farms –
all the signs will be foreign. I
slip through a copse, passing a pig
joyously rooting for truffles.

[1984]

FROM

A FLAME IN YOUR HEART

(1986)

'I don't want to set
The world on fire
I just want to start
A flame in your heart.'

1

We were carrying our dance shoes,
keeps them good, saves our corns.
Darkness, miles, and not so much as a match.
Rose yanked me into a ditch. Too late,
it glanced my leg. Huge car, soft and fast.
Never slowed at all. 'Near thing!' she says.
Neither light nor sound, could have been dreaming.
I was crying. Rose rubbed the dirt and bruises.
I stared into the blackout. They just purr on happily.
Stared again. Saw red. It dawned on me. The war, I mean.

2

The moment a kiss comes to an end,
we open our eyes, read consent in one another's
and kiss again, more forcefully,
we could be other lovers. Is it when
I'm mesmerised by the slow unwinding
bandage in my hand that you grow distant
from the pilots' room, feel us, dancing?
Till someone digs your ribs, exclaims
'Come on, mate, your deal!'
Sometimes we just step outside, as lovers will
for a breath of air, those narrow halls
where a dance-band's marking time.

3

What you said about being shot down –
I think I know (I shouldn't compare). At the bus stop
someone was reading the news. I strained
to see the list, you know, of names,
caught sight of what looked like 'Appleton'. The rain
came on, drops landing on the page
spread through. He folded it away
before I could see if it was true.

There was a sort of quiet feeling, as if
wardrobes and pianos were falling silently downstairs,
before the plummet, what happened you said
when you were hit, how the ground rears up like a rabid mare.
I couldn't stop falling down this spiral pit, expecting
to meet rock, or the sea. All the time I was changing sheets.
Jane was kind, though I didn't say. When she spoke,
it was like a wireless playing to an empty Mess.

It was four hours before I saw a paper. The name
was Applethwaite. Remember when you pushed
the stick into the hand of the blind man who'd
dropped it, and was panicky? I felt like him,
like you lads when you regain control,
lift the aircraft out of its spin, get the earth
beneath again. Len, I can't help but imagine
this crumpled shape: your plane; Mrs Applethwaite.

4

She scans the same horizon
from the other side
and I can almost touch her hands,
her kiss falls just too light.

Fraulein, one of us will burn tonight.
The other will waltz with an airman,
listen to the day's war news.
And I can almost reach her hands.

5

We don't have seasons, we just repeat
the same on a groaning train of men
who get discharged at the other end.
Under our hands, nothing changes.

I want to be a Land Girl with itching eyes,
I want you to see me rise from a wheat field,
stretch to ease an aching back, drive tractors
through orchards, let the sun slap me, sweat,
let the grime smeared on my brow run into furrows
that will turn into wrinkles one day. Not yet.
Let us girls throw our arms around each others' necks,
smell cattle and soil, give that direct
feminine leer to trucks passing full
of lewd soldiers. Let me cut down a harvest.
I want to take tea-breaks lying flat on my back,
to accept without question whatever pictures occur
in the clouds. Just let me get these
damn stockings off. I'd walk home at twilight,
cry with the cows if I wanted,
instead of holding it back like a show of bad temper.

Out in the fields is death at its best:
owls pick off the slowest mice, moles'
skin-and-bone dangle from fences. I want
growth: dirt on my delicate hands.

6

The moon has set. At last
the ducks I watched asleep
at the edges of their pond,
fat and warm, are stirring.
You ought to know: I'm very late,

and sway between a silly pride,
a need: to grow large and round
as if by magic, as if I knew
I contained the world
and was besotted. Then fear:

I hold my head. My world will split,
the two halves fall and
gently rock, like cradles.
I waken early, listen for my familiar
ache. Should you wonder,

that is, not want to know,
count me among your 'possibles'.
We'll go to London. Blend
with the other widows there, real
or feigned. I shan't use your name.

I shan't even send this letter.
Not until I know. This, somehow, is my show.

7

Blood? Only port wine, suddenly drunk,
who's that giggling? Coughing on dust,
a stairway pointing up to the sky
naked and rude, terribly funny.

And a sharp tearing. I'm swearing,
there's fizzing and gurgling from severed
pipes, cuts on my legs, all the bells ringing
my head, here come people. Dust settles down
like a sigh. It all becomes clear.

Sharp as blades.
'I've torn my dress!' Laughing again.
The old barman who was chatting me up,
he's weeping over a stone. I mutter
'come now' so arch 'there's a war on, you know',

digging like a dog for a bone. Blue
to the lips, and I hear the word
he's about to utter, plea and command:
'Nurse?' Saw an arm. I thought:
'That's the last time I talk to strangers
in pubs. Should say I'm a typist.'

8

maybe she didn't die
        honestly   I walked away
all the others came running
        as much future follows from that
I didn't save her
        as would had I stayed
          (not for her not
Despise me? I shudder at 'murder'
        some kid over the river might
        tell her grandchild how the shockwaves
        rattled the windows
I have not cold eyes
        there I am fiddling with an eternity ring
        telling my son about 'during the war'
Forgive? (Ask a fighter
forgiveness
        the actions we don't
        just as effective
for not saving a life?
        how aware we become
        of dead friends, at parties.

        it's getting easier talking to you.

9

Walking home to mother's,
the church one side of the river
on the other: the village.
And I'm laughing, pointing
to no one that the bridge
you must cross to the graveyard
and the country beyond
had been bombed. Gone,
but for the supports inclined
toward one another
and the river coursing through stones.

10

There is darkness everywhere
outside the circle of our lamp.
I'm lucid and awake, it's the middle
of the night and the only thing I felt
this hour before was dread. But
there are no monsters any more,
we've outgrown them, the space they left
is full again – of something else, not fear.
I used to hear them whispering if I'd done
something wrong. They've quite gone.
What woke me then? The moon can't penetrate
the blackout blinds; Len's sound:
dreaming of maps and aerodromes, and
keeping his options closed.
Except this one. Should I wake and tell him?
See him overawed, and wondering
'is it right?' It is. I know.

11 *War Widow*

You know I keep the photograph
beside my bed. It gathers glances
like I could
when I swayed my way amongst airmen.

The trees behind you are still
fresh, your face never changes.

My stocking seams aren't quite so straight.
My uniform's returned. You wear yours
somewhere,
caught in a snapshot while you slept.

FROM

THE WAY WE LIVE

(1987)

I.

Clearances

The wind sucks clouds. In the indrawn breath
grass bends and nods, like Mandarins.
The sun hunches, and begins to set no sooner
than it's risen. This
depopulated place! Where moorland birds
repeat a sound, like copper, beaten.
The very moon imagines things –
a desert dusk, with itself as scimitar...
As the wind keeps up, closer than
I've heard my name in...how long?
and the dark coheres; an old idea
returns again, the prodigal friend:
of leaving: for Szechwan, or Persia.

Bosegran

Everything is natural, from the cotton summer
dress to the horizon; a natural illusion.
In the water of the cove, with its plates
of green weed fixed and shifting like continents,
is some irritation – an object discarded from a boat
or the few white houses on the shore
looking out to sea. The sea lies open as an eye.

Alone in all the world one is playing.
A seal, fluid and dark, has the plastic colonised,
round her like a jacket. I watched them tumble
and dive, and water cuff rock
till the sea took the colour of the sky. To what end?
– but 'why?' is just salt blown in the mind's eye.
The seal delights. The sun climbs higher as the world goes about.

Poem for a Departing Mountaineer

Regarding the skyline longingly
(curved as a body, my own, I desire you)
where ink-coloured cloud masses
and rolls on the ridge,
I pick out silhouettes. Deer
dolmen, trees, perhaps tombs
raised through the bracken and weird
midsummer nights by the ancients.
Or men. I can't discern, and mustn't wonder
whether the figures are vibrant, stone,
setting out hunched under loads
or turning home. I must be distant,
draw the curtains for bed,
and leave them, like you who left
with your grave-goods strapped to your back
alone to the lowering cloud.

Duet

I am the music of the string duet
in the Métro, and my circumstances,
nowadays, are music too: travelling
the underground like women's scent, or happiness.
Again and again I discover that I love you
as we navigate round Châtelet
and hear once more the music. It's found its way
through passages to where I least expect,
and when you kiss me, floods me.
The trains come in, whine out again,
the platforms fill and empty:
a movement regular as your heart's
beat, mine as lively as the melody.

Julian of Norwich

Everthing I do I do for you.
Brute. You inform the dark
inside of stones, the winds draughting in

from this world and that to come,
but never touch me.
You took me on

but dart like a rabbit into holes
from the edges of my sense
when I turn, walk, turn.

*

I am the hermit whom you keep
at the garden's end, but I wander.
I am wandering in your acres

where every step, were I
attuned to sense them,
would crush a thousand flowers.

(Hush, that's not the attitude)
I keep prepared a room and no one comes.
(Love is the attitude)

*

Canary that I am, caged and hung
from the eaves of the world
to trill your praise.

He will not come.
Poor bloodless hands, unclasp.
Stiffened, stone-cold knees, bear me up.

(And yet, and yet, I am suspended
in his joy, huge and helpless
as the harvest moon in a summer sky.)

Lepidoptery

So you stay
up at night mounting angels
you've caught
on the leaves of a book,
arranging the wings
in precise (be honest,
lifeless) imitations of flight.

You prefer the
perfect collection.
Most angels are mortal;
they look vague
and benign, as sexlessness ought.

We should pity
the fluttering creatures
who gamble their lives for
a chance to be
shadows, however frantic and huge.

Real angels laugh
in the presence of light.
They can taste ether
high on the wind.

I want one of those,
the immortals, the
threatening, true,
proclamatory angels, the blinding,
the kind lusted after by
equinox gales. I
dream of sustaining one, breathing.

Peter the Rock

The last trumpet of sunlight blows over the sea,
he moves high on the cliff, sure of his grace
and raises an arm. The fingers connect.
He pulls up and leans out, hair falling straight toward earth.

He tells me he dreams about nothing
but falling, though we sleep on the sand.
His arms always round me, golden hair
spilled over my face. That mysterious injury
torn in his shoulders: 'I told you, I fell.'

Even in kissing you feel for holds,
grip through to bone.
It doesn't surprise me, I do it myself,
enrage you with symbol, the meaning of things.
You practise moves and hate gestures,
God-talk with vengeance, imperfect shoulders.

I change the tapes. He drives, and will go on denying
into the night. There is nothing
but rock and the climbing of rock under the sun.
Which I say is falling and setting behind us, unfolded,
flashed in the wing mirrors, golden, your skin tone.

II.

KARAKORAM HIGHWAY

*I tuck'd my trowser-ends in my boots and went
and had a good time*
WALT WHITMAN

1

Stop thinking now, and put on your shoes.
Those cobwebs below, sprinkled with dew:
those are the villages. You
are a blip in someone's long night.
About to be born. Into the light.
Set your watches, we're falling.
There's no friction in flying or thinking ahead.

Wheels have engaged, scorched on the runway
So it's going to be hot, is it? All coming true.

2

I have seen the devil; he was baking chapati
in an all night roadhouse on the Karakoram Highway.
Flames in his hair, a pit oven, a hook.
Soft talking somnolent takers of tea
and a three-legged dog. Hissing of lanterns
incensed by night. Angora blackness!
Trucks at the roadside, patient and glinting.
Engines revving, our bus backs out,
tinkles, sways. Give the devil his due, let's be going.

The most vivid dream from the darkest sleep:
our headlamps glare on a tanker's rump, all painted
with a trucker's idyll. Green concupiscent hills
trailing in rivers, lazy sun, and one truck,
this one, back-end painted with a trucker's idyll...
we overtake, throwing up dust in the tanker's face.

Shaken down. A grotto-bus.
Jocular groans, the chuckling of the damned, the stoned
absorbed in fairy-lights, intense designs,
luminous bells, talismen,
Aladdin's cavern of rucksacks and ice axes.
Other buses squeeze past like fat rouged tarts
in chrome tiaras,
full of oddly angled limbs, charmed lives;
nothing so Asian as night.

The tailor alone with his sewing machine,
roadside caffs, rows of lit up shacks, silver
stitches in the cloth of night.
Men who'll never meet have seen
our bus, it filled a moment
like the vision on the tanker; or perhaps
they're sustaining us, handing us
each to the next as they look up, look down
at their nocturnal metal work, or basketry.

3

The wave breaks on the smallest stone,
rolls on. Dawn as eternal occurrence;
always someplace. Darkness, dusk, day,
seem immutable as the poplar trees
that make a place. It's permanent
midnight at that check-point, or where
the herd and goats turned to stare
forever half-light, soft as chicks.
Unmanned border of night and day, we rumble on
toward the sun – a tiny cut in orange peel,
sharp sting of smell – Ah, breakfast!

4

At the sharp end of the gorge;
the bridge. Like a single written word
on vast and rumpled parchment. Bridge.
The statement of man in landscape.

And how they guard it.
Drifts of people in either bank
like brackets, knowing it can crash
to the river in a mangled scribble
and be erased.
They write it up again, single syllable
of construction
shouted over the canyon.

5

And all the driver wants is eye-drops
before he straightens up the bus, commits us.
At least malevolence concedes your existence;
worse is indifference, power and indifference.
The river brawls beneath us, self-obsessed,
narcissistic. Wheels turn, turn again, full weight.
The bridge starts to undulate and we're hanging
out of windows half-roads over the Indus,
grinning at each other, impotent, enlightened.
The world grew tight.

It must have been about then we first saw the mountains.

6

Emotion is human, the foothills brown,
the valley floor very low. We haven't slept.
Our thoughts are slow and wide.
The mind can turn its own death in its hand,
chat blythly about mountains, until
the last moment, that appalling rise that ends
in total unemotional blue.
First sight of the summits, distant
and almost transparent, like glass.
Call it distance, not menace. White, not frightening:
emotion is human, is returned to the human
along with your life. A slight
clash of terror, you lower your eyes.
The sun reflected from glass,
more fearsome than glass in itself.

7

It's earthly and brown, deep inside canyons.
Stones at the roadside:
'Here rock fell on men', 'men fell to the river'
and the river and rock were unmoved
being river and rock.
He takes it fast.
Some nameless white mountain
has closed off the end of the canyon.
The walls grow taller, the river hysterical.
He brakes, hauls the wheel. No talking.
No colour but brown –
except in the mind. It's been many hours.
Fear passes out into long passive blue,
a slight smile – there is nothing at all we can do.
And the sky widens, the canyon gives out
to a strange sort of kingdom
and the first hanging village swings in.

8

The year's greening crop spilled
down dull unaltering rock like the tail
of a bird. We can recognise this:

that crops yellow, get cut,
turn in on themselves over winter, head under wing,
and begin to feel like ourselves again.

Suspended villages, terraces
layered wide in the movement of scythes,
the unthreatening gesture of sowing.

9

Maybe this is as close as we'll get to the mountains.

Squatting on the steps of the K2 Motel
another wretched K2 cigarette.
No great altitude. Clouds sit like headaches
on the walls of this desolate vast arena,
gather round like the Skardu men
with chapati-hats, their clothes
come through dust-storms down the bazaar.

Someone's cooking. The bus has turned back.
Silence and space fall strangely on us all;
leaned against walls with the gear.
Some look at the finances, some at a half-baked
patch of grass, waiting for food
and the day after tomorrow.

Some just look at the hills, keep looking,
tapping plastic spoons onto plastic plates.

10

That day was raised, a song of a note
from the clapped-out engine. Headwind, hot
in our eyes. Streams, children
splashing down to the roadside, wave,
flowers jammed into their hands 'K2 going?' and
the corn is yellow banked up the hillside.
Lost in dust. This jeep-ride takes us to mountains.

Maybe I'm drowning and this is my life: flashes
on birds' wings, head shaking delight,
beasts in the shade, greenery, embroidery,
women in shawls with the same limbless sway
as a poplar. Grubby babies on roofs, goats,
yaks in a farmyard. Here and passed.
Tree-tips high against blue.
Berries fell to our laps – is this Eden? –
we ate them. Mohammed Ali threw his hat,
caught it, laughed, and
an old dame up an apricot tree
surveyed her river, her valley. High state
of movement, track climbing to meet us
appearing, like everything else at a distance
to blend into heat, to shimmer like mercury.
The shimmer of joy on the face of uncertainty.

11

Boys drive down the yaks from high pasture
secure them with latches. Darkness comes rising
from rivers, underneath walls
with the light floating up on its back.
Our village rolls itself up in a blanket,
a burst of coughing or song. At length
I untie my boots and leave them outside
under the moon, Orion from home.
Then zip the flaps.
Such fine skin between us and the wide rolling night:
no one feels fearful. Not myself, not the yaks
asleep in their cellars, bovine and black.

12

The palm of a crystal-gazer's hand
night lifts away, things become defined:
this is our world for a time, these its colours.

Tea fires burn down to embers.
Under the trees they're strapping up baggages,
untying goats. Light fills like a cup

so we pick up our packs and the rhythm of walk.
Keep walking while the world remains sharp
as rock grasped intently,

as the percussion of boots on the track.
While the river's throughout like a sense of myself,
before foot-slogging with thought

gives out to no thought,
to heat and hours mounting like cliffs.
Come noon, we're vacant as goats.

Pain and sun only as undergone.
Until evening, when all things are dismantled:
loads, mountains, trees,

a bit of banter and food,
and we sleep by the track, which continues,
with the sound of the river all night.

III.

Risk

Your own death smiles out from you.
He is not evil, does not
leer, stink, terrify
old women, old women
are not so easily scared
as young. He is there, unseen, within,
like skeleton.
And in your absence I live alone,
don't keep household ghosts,
I am mistress. But you oscillate
inside my mind
from man to fool to hero to child.
I fear grief, I fear myself
alone with him –
he is a scummy mess we dabble in,
greases our fingers
and stains our hands,
like nicotine.

Aunt Janet's Museum

What can be gained by rushing these things?
Huddle in from the rain, compose ourselves, let
a forefinger rest on the bell button which
requests kindly 'p   s'. We wait, listening
to bus tyres on rain say *hush* and *west*.
People hurry behind us, we wait,
for shuffling inside the door,
tumbling locks, and admission to dark.

One after the other we make up the stair.
No one looks back, we know what's there,
fear what lies ahead may disappear. Could we
forget these ritual sounds, or alter their order?
Scuffle of feet on the narrow stair,
the alcove, the turn where
pallid light faints through the glass of the doors.

Let it be right. She takes the handle, still
softly exclaiming over our height, and lets her weight
drop it. The click of the latch. She pushes the door
till the shop bell above gives a delicate ting.
Sounds of inside step forward. The faraway drill
of bells warning the kitchen, and the fallible clock.

Havers

She once went to Girvan on horseback
it's said. Wind from the hillsides
through her hair and its mane, sheep
on the roadside. Havers. Her hair
never felt breezes, caught to her neck
like grey fleece to wire. She appears
and reappears out of the gloom
on her way down to greet us, tiny and silent
as a jet flying through cloud.
How dare we bring inside our knowledge of skies?
We take her hands: saint's bones, kiss her cheek,
thinking of flaky grey parchment
of past summers' wasp-nests,
and hurry to proffer our gift – something blue.

The Latter-day Noah

At last there's industry, heaven-sent work,
batter and clang from the shipyard.
Horses are snorting, pulling in wood, pitch,
hammers. Tell me, what is our cargo?
He nodded out of the window. 'Archetypes.'
And where do we take them? He went on staring.
'Just sail. And keep sailing. Sail over the
edge if you must.' We'll be killed! 'On the contrary
you might find an island.'
With the tigers and sharks?
'I'll send you a sign.' What'll that be?
'A rainbow.' Another arc? You're obsessed!
'You'll all live there forever.'
You mean frogs are immortal?
'The greenfly are... Forms. The cats are not
actual. You must sail to the heavens...' What?
'The transcendent.' But that isn't charted!
'True, but it's near and very like this,'
he said, reaching out to the window,
touching the rain through the glass.

The Philosopher Extemporises in the Fairground

Should we accept the solar system
is, so, in fact, to speak
a Ferris wheel,

(albeit Royal, Televised, Electric and
Noted for Pleasing Young and Old
in Safety and Comfort)

and we are shackled by luck
into this turquoise cart
and here secured

by a tattooed gypsy who
sets the wheel rolling
only to leave

to watch his son walk the nebulous
waltzers, like some casual
Christ on water?

Then. He is neglecting us.
We are slowing down.
Our sky blue vehicle

may well attain that coveted
space, point the highest,
nearest the stars.

We may well sway above
the lurid art
and flashes

and little golden fishes.
Never, however, the less
we thinkers descend

and must assume we will meet
with no greater end than a jerk
of our tinker's thumb.

God Almighty the First Garden Made

How did I get where I am today?
How did I get where I am today? Lass,
I hauled mesel up by me own boot straps. See
all I started out with was seventeen jars of bluebells,
and were on funerals for years. Then I 'ad this idea...

For fenugreek, and marigolds, then along came the anemones,
down the mart at dawn, I bought in job lots of greenery,
expanded in a small way with a little blend for England
(hollyhocks and foxgloves and Cox's orange pippins).

Secured an export deal for cacti, but I got me fingers burned
on nettles. They'd no sooner got laburnum seeds
then they're clamouring for wheat. I gave it, too; albeit
with poppies. (I'm not a hard man, I hear deputations, Sundays.)

T'Word spread. Travellers went to Africa with suchlike
samples of exotica as malachite, antelopes, and a tropical strain
of thunder. Then t'was Lapsang Souchong and iridescent bees,
BUT I never forgot me roots, oh no! (Ah me! them Baobab trees!)

I'm getting on. I'll be calling it a day soon,
and handing over to me son. I just fidget
with hedgerows now, do a small line in peas. I like
to put me feet up on me footstool, sunny afternoons,
and cut me own toenails to meet demand for crescent moons.

Petrol

Sketch in the background: pre-dawn
in winter, snow on the hillsides,
marsh: brown-green, a winding
lochside road,
black ice.

It could have been
so much worse. No one was hurt.
As if you can care about
alternative universes
when this one gives trouble enough. O

that bonny smashed-up power-steering,
disc-brakes, axle,
front nearside suspension; no more
easy overnighting, end
of spinning our cash into petrol.

We must haul ourselves
out of the mire with help
from the keeper's tractor and none
whatsoever from the governors of fate,
who look down

on the scratch-marks, and smile.
Who look down on the petrol
spilled on the roadside
and smile.
It's business. It's tough.

The engine we'll resurrect, someday.
Tonight, hit the whisky
till we're split out through the spectrum:
as readily consumed, as volatile,
as figures etched in petrol.

The Way We Live

Pass the tambourine, let me bash out praises
to the Lord God of movement, to Absolute
non-friction, flight, and the scarey side:
death by avalanche, birth by failed contraception.
Of chicken tandoori and reggae, loud, from tenements,
commitment, driving fast and unswerving
friendship. Of tee-shirts on pulleys, giros and Bombay,
barmen, dreaming waitresses with many fake-gold
bangles. Of airports, impulse, and waking to uncertainty,
to strip-lights, motorways, or that pantheon –
the mountains. To overdrafts and grafting

and the fit slow pulse of wipers as you're
creeping over Rannoch, while the God of moorland
walks abroad with his entourage of freezing fog,
his bodyguard of snow.
Of endless gloaming in the North, of Asiatic swelter,
to launderettes, anecdotes, passions and exhaustion,
Final Demands and dead men, the skeletal grip
of government. To misery and elation; mixed,
the sod and caprice of landlords.
To the way it fits, the way it is, the way it seems
to be: let me bash out praises – pass the tambourine.

THE AUTONOMOUS REGION

(1993)

1

O a great downward lurch of the heart, as though
he dreamily stepped off an unexpected kerb;
Fa-hsien in the city. He says:
    'Need all situations be resolvable/ resolved?'
or
    'Is there a high pass over the mountains?'

and hopes/hopes not. Rumour flits the city
like bats, flits the city like bats by night,
rumours on the lips of running tea-boys,
delivered on the hour, on trays like tea.
    And the rumours say yes, the rumours say no.

And with a great shout and a creak
the shoulders of 100 youths
pulled the wingèd city gates, and all
that were going walked or rode
out to the desert before them.

2

Fires burning in the bellies of yurts at the day's end:
beside a river, such a clear stream there, with a fish.
If he could return he'd return to that river
as the sun rose like a fish behind mountains
and the stream, cleared to crystal, foretold.
A purple range to East and to West,
he remarks:
                    'Not a few have turned back.
Promise or rumour without author or source
ever keeps us moving, against the way
of the small clear river' – which is to say: uphill.
Devotions over, the ice mountains'
jagged edges met his gaze. He smiles, 'Life!
Wo! *That* straggling caravan.' Then: 'But what to you
are the ramblings of Fa-hsien?' Begins to walk.

3

Walked beneath the power lines
(sagging like pigs' bellies in the sun)
between the desert graves and gravel mounds,
scared the crows with open black beaks, walked
abandoned tar-barrels, wiped the sweat
and wondered aloud:
                    'How did this begin?'
just one tiny act: he'd dropped the keys back
thro' the letter-box.
And though molten tar got stuck to his feet,
all in all he thought it rather wonderful.
He said to himself:
                    'Well, is there?'
when, to others insisted:
                    'There *is*.' Secretly, he loved
the way his lips cracked, loved
to feel his head spin, loved
to cough the dust and consider himself
a journeyman, a-journeying.

4

Meanwhile, in another place,
the princess (travelling, travelling)
breaks the Sun-Moon Mirror and weeps.

A strong-willed woman and resolute,
she knows when to weep.

5 *The princess breaks the Sun-Moon Mirror*

As if a city child knows his heart
can take no more of this awful thudding,
and in a cellar stale and hot,
black and breathy
as his granny's lap
escapes his mother's grasp
and makes by alleys and deserted wynds
to the splintering gates,
hears the roar,
knows all's lost
           so opens them.

                  'What I will I own' says the princess.
                  Surveys her perfect world.
                  'A life thrown round my shoulders
                  luxurious as fur; my heart twitches
                  like a dreaming cat.'

Dear maid running
with sodden clothes clung to her like children
whose rain-soaked face is like a sister's,
whose company is a clear pool
on a deep and secret river
grasp each other horrified as flowers
and cannot even yell above the wind
sees the mirror smashed at the princess' tiny feet
and on her lips
the beginnings
of a terrible
and mischievous
smile.

6

Carved dragons framed the door, fierce and delicate
our house-on-stilts. Creepers chased like monkeys
round our high, half-hidden walls whose gates
opened onto tree-tops; streams
flashing to the village pleased us first. I loved
the tremors that occasionally bucked
our youthful gorge as if a finger
traced its spine. My colour then
was mother-of-pearl; my bed and bedding,
nails, the combs that held my ornate hair...
I'd lean on the verandah, breathe jasmine
air, lean on the verandah, lean and fancy.
But I loved it best when snow came, the distant world
would soothe its troubled self into a pearl.

7

'The shattered windscreen splits the sun
to a glass chrysanthemum. A few dead buildings
the road's cast up like shells. Your turn.'
'There's nothing here for us,
just a couple of nomads' yurts. Darling
this is *gulag*.' Wen Cheng
chucked a bottle from the window,
watched it splash to bits with a certain
satisfaction. 'What,' she asked
'are those sacks out there,
ranked like the dumb soldiers of the terracotta army?'
(those that were new were full of desert dust,
those that were old had rot)
'It's the labour of the people,' said the maid
and lit a cigarette.

8

After three days in the desert he came to a spring.
Laughing, grins, 'sweat, mortals, crowd
like wing-torn moths about me'; it was
all charm, the winning smile, laughed
until it fell away in channels; the channels
run to villages, are disciples with news
of glories and miracles sparkling on their lips.
Harvests are delivered fathered by disciples.
For a short time he took this in.
                    Then it was back to the desert.

Sits a lassie in red scarf,
wi her heid in her hauns, her heid
achin wi the weicht o so much saun
the weicht o the desert that waits every morn
an blackly dogs her back.

And road-builders watch their passing, turn
like weary sunflowers tracking the sun.

9

So said the maid into her dictaphone:
'Times she'd sit and hum discordant notes
above her walkman, growl
'I'm drowning in this desert' another hour
and she'd mutter:
                    a girl
                         could get
                                 bored.

Wen Cheng's
            acting up, yes
she's wilding in the dining-car
I hear the
            smash of crockery, the waiter
swirling like a matador and fair enough
it's 2 a.m. (Beijing). Now comes she lurching:
'Pass the phrase-book, darling,
let's have a sesh with these dear Uygar boys.'
The Uygar stare at this phenomenon, but
they've tired of their comic books,
give toothless grins and pass the bottle.

So the train bends on. Come the day
the boys and her still playing
paper/stone/knife to some serious arak.
It's a lengthy journey, it's a battlefield;
sprawling bodies stir and find their
rightful owners. A hard-bit woman
sweeps the husks and fag-ends out onto the track.

The princess rises with all her grace and lurches
down the corridor, the boys discuss
in guttural tongues. She's back:
this time announced
'It's not unusual for golden-hairs
to lie where
Chinese only spit.' '?' I said
'Read it some place,' she replied and
took another swig. Her last.'

The party journeyed on for 15 days
in a south-westerly direction
over a difficult, precipitous and dangerous
road, the side of the mountain
being like a stone wall
10,000 feet in height.

10

Unbeknown to them, Fa-hsien,
riding hobo on the box-car
sees the desert change miraculous to plain.
He fancies in the sheep-dogs' bark
a hidden 'yes!' and doesn't half
admire how the nomads ride,
so splits his time, between, on one hand,
attending to the scenery
he's dragged across,
and on the other, learning to divine.

Learning to divine his own future.
He's laying low, he's two days out
heart-in-mouth and hiding from the police
and diesel fumes. It's a truck-of-lead
and slow. The sky's detonated
blue across the day; he stares it out
and hopes, conversely fears and knows.
He feels quite sick. It's worth it.

Swags and swathes of hills billowing o
as a child he dreamed of sailing; the sailing hills;
he hears his heart shanty and shepherds
call like bosuns.
The prayer-flags yearn like full-rigged ships
to quit this witness, earth. He knows
already he's too far slipped
to make the leap ashore.
Aye, it's strange quiver; and he knows
himself an arrow already shot the bow.
He cries, tells himself, as if he didn't know
It's worth it, worth it, worth it.

His bed is hard, his smell
a travel-musk of months through teeming villages.
The walls of course are stained, the sheet
he almost envies: old, plain.

He rises, ties his top-knot, wanders
to the boiler-room, with his
double-happiness thermos flask,
noting
     every vessel can be broken, filled,
and he is empty, these days. Not old
as the sun-lines round his eyes suggest
which eyes have seen:
         many things out of strong places
et cetera. And who knows what his robe conceals:
tattoos, a bleeding heart.

*

There's roads and there are one-horse-towns
and any climb out of hamlet, gorge or wilderness
he looks in wonder,
to fellow travellers he replies:
'What wisdom have I gathered? None!
That's my tuppence worth', walks on.
'Threw it in a ditch and walk unburdened.'

And also in the ditch, a dog, days dead, ignored.
'I've lied and vowed at umpteen altars,
and know I can be
                utterly deceived.
Perhaps still am.'

At the thin black line of shade at a truckstop
while they fix the fan-belt
and there's no water
he'll bring out yarrow-stalks, divine.
And sometimes, walking alone, he finds
the centre of his being, flinches,
for it's nowt
                but an alms bowl.
Waiting at a roadside, he scratches the dust
with a stick, finds: more dust.
In the hot shade of some godforsaken Xinjiang bunkhouse
remembers the river and the fish.

(o monk, whither do you wander?
to garner wisdom and bring scripture home)

Fine horsewomen both and a long time travelling.
Wen Cheng bends low and adjusts the stirrup.
Something tells her this is the border: a breath of wind
from the dark and jagged mountains
a circus of secrets in the valley at her feet.

Nights, and the tents glow in a river bend,
the keepers of secrets
                together in cliques –
master brewers growing merry round a camp-fire;
thin-faced glass-makers trickle silt
                between their fingers,
the silk-workers guard their covered baskets.
And Wen Cheng could read the marks of darkness.
O rumour, they have no paper, beer, script.
Sometimes she wonders
                what kind of place it is she's going,
kicks the horse and turns down before nightfall.

Like the others these days she talks most about the future;
out in the night they're starting to communicate;
secrets revealed and revealed amongst themselves.

We crossed the watershed. A small stream
ran with us down the mountain;
a thumb of rainbow marked the sky.
At the doors of yurts
women and girls wiped their brows
and waved as they churned
summer to its yellow end, a sound
like oars
               on a still and distant loch.

In a purse the mirror's shards
tied from her waist, tinkled most attractively
as we rode; smashed, she sighed
             into this/ not this
             like a common
                   bottle
                   of bitter beer.

And holding the dancing horse on a tight rein
twisted back, hair joyously undone
I told her 'we are tense vessels, each contain
all the energy required for change'
which made her laugh, and I knew
that if her robes indeed concealed
             a little lady's
             pearl-handled pistol
it was for nought
but shooting locks off boxes, prison cells et cetera.

As yaks gathered at the fanks,
like an inhaled breath, buttercups
at their patient hooves
hardened their hearts
against the night. Our running dogs
sniffed a hint of snow,
on the golden sunset
where a lark's black flight
leapt and leapt
like a telegraph wire
on a straight road.

At the shore of a loch called Qinghai we rested,
hobbled the horses and let them graze
the sweet wild pasture.

13

Fa-hsien, cross-legged in a light rain,
takes his tin spectacle case,
      watches the first print he ever made
(on a lonely shore)
              wash away.
Though desert dust still clings to his hems
he has bathed fresh and clean
in his joyous lake,
and now his hand and cards have changed,
reveal
a hanker for his ain folk,
      his auld hert follows suit.

14

When we reached the lake, pure and shining,
like a mirror of itself
in sheer joy we jumped down, swirled round and round
so our clothes belled out and graced the silt
with a circle which we defined:
Our space
Mine
which I hadn't done since we were bairns
in gym-shoes.

(and I recalled the last town we'd passed,
en fête, where jugglers and acrobats
called a crowd around
but its centre was their stage.
In that dirty township
                    I hid my face
behind a fluttering fan,
of Queens and Aces,
so by the angry hiss of a
hurricane lamp
in the back of a chop-house
lost and won a pretty sum
and some I tossed to a blind beggar,
some a pick-pocket filched
and three gold coins I saved
for out the corner
                    of my eye,
behind my winning hand I'd seen
a wandering holy-man and part-time diviner.

Whose little fire rose scented
smoke into the sky, along the shore.

The joyous lake

turned coral, jasper in the gloaming,
a heron beat its languid wings,
though he called them back, shore-birds
flashed, were gone;

a woman in silhouette
arranged some silvered shards
on a granite boulder
then played a reed pipe
over the water

and with these folk Fa-hsien
devoured a meal,
shared travellers' nonsense,
risqué jokes,

until the mirror showed
the shepherd moon,
its scattered flock of stars.

Then I asked:
will we come this way again, this smiling lake?
And though the princess laid off playing
turned her back, we could feel
she was all ears when he warned
some things may never be resolved
then studied my upturned hand.

My cross-hatched palm: lines straight
as a cormorant's flight
                              like an arrow shot
slow over the silent loch

said all that was past was lost
and there was everything to come

Set a stout hert tae a stey brae
                he winked (a wink that showed
he wasn't so old he couldn't
follow home a twisting road
with a click of his heels,
wouldn't resist
                a backward glance
to see who followed this ridiculous dance
through many people's many tongues.)

*

A sharp and sudden wind
forced between loch and sky
as if from under an ill-fitting door

as the princess tossed the coins
through heads and tails

and even she who'd snorted 'truth?
a game of spot-the-ball'

grew serious
as bracken shook, horses stamped
the troubled loch sent waves ashore,

scattered the diviner's cards,
our faces there.

Calm: and Fa-hsien took a twig
drew in the dust the coins' revelation

spoke to a place at the centre of us all:
the fire's core,

described a future in a measured tone:
if she'd be true

to her mirror
cracked, her inner loch, that humble heart,

the great force of that keen wind: her name
would be revered.

*

15

We saw him once more: in the dusty dawn
a distant home-turned figure
jaunty as a fiddler
down the loch-side dirt track.

As we saddled up, ready for the last push,
wondering again what kind of place it was
we rode toward
                    with a new resolve.

16 *The Panchen Lama rides from Lhasa to Kumbum*
(A thousand miles in a single night)

Now the sky is saddled with stars,
a saddle of stars thrown over the hills' back;
night is a horse leaping the mountains,
night is a nomad shifted by morning,
the Panchen Lama rides hard out of Lhasa
low and clung to the horse's mane,
clings to the mane strung like a comet,
and clear of the darkened back-streets chants
to the ready ear, pale as a conch shell
the thousandth tantra's thousandth cycle,
and horse and Lama quit their earthly forms.

That night a wind crossed snow and pasture:
ruffled the feathers of sleeping rivers,
whirled like a cloak round the shoulders of mountains.
The plateau of Tibet
stretched away like an oil-dark painting
to the grass-land, where in tethered yurts
families wrapped in yaks-wool, slept;
and warm-flanked yaks shifted in their dreaming,
and certain dogs
who opened their jaws to the flying hoof-beat
with an invisible gesture of the Lama's hand
were silenced and charmed.

So for a thousand miles:
till the sun coaxed the world to open like a daisy;
splashed gold on the roofs on the gold-rooved monastery,
of the far side of the precious and protecting hill
at will assumed their mortal shape,
and the youngest boy-monk who rushed from the temple,
his face as round as a gong of wonder
to touch the robe, grab the reins, receive a blessing
and though that boy lived to be a hundred
he always swore
the Panchen Lama
winked.

(This is no story, desperate and apocryphal,
the horse is rumoured to be divine.)

17

As the Lama rode to the golden roofs
so the rays of the sun lead to the golden sun
so the wild stories come together
round a burning campfire
and the pewter path over the grassland
is a straight track. So we are come. We turn over the stones
of the past as if reasons
and beginnings scuttled beneath,
and the rumours we repeat to ourselves
converge on truth.
The desert spoke in false voices tho' alluring,
but we can close the door softly and be gone,
with what we own
                    we must carry and bear.
And our horse mayn't be divine,
we must ride it and be astonished and glad
to arrive at a clutter of gold roofs
cupped in a valley:
with a scented tree
whose every leaf
shimmers with the face of the divine.

18 *For Paola*

A boomin echo doon the corridor,
her door's the only ane open

lik a shell, an a wumman sweepin:
saft soun, wings.

A licht-bulb, hingit fi the ceilin
by a short cord.

A slever o gless in the oose
an a black hair. she telt me

they've killed 5000 people in Beijing.
Nou this wumman's haunin her gear

brushes an pens, her worn claes
for me tae cairry. But she'd a bin waitin

when they cam, chewin her gum
blawn them a bubble size o China.

This is a place your friens disappear:
trust naebody. Luve a.

The smearit wa's o a concrete room,
a wumman sweepin.

19 *Sang o the blin beggar*

This is the dynasty o wickitness –
grieve agin the nicht an howl wi dugs

Great buildins murn thir ugliness –
dugs are scroungin politicians born again

the stars grow dangerous; they ken the script
o constellation's no thir ain

Folk that talk lik rivers o risin
will be swept awa tae gutters lik the rain

o this dynasty o wickitness
grieve agin the night and howl wi dugs.

20 *Xiahe*

Abune the toon o Xiahe
a thrast monastery,
warn lik a yowe's tuith.

The sun gawps at innermaist
ingles o wa's.
Secret as speeders

folk hae criss-crosst a saucht
seedit i the yird flair
wi rags o win blawn prayer.

Xiahe. Wave droonin wave
on a pebbly shore,
the *ahe* o machair, o slammach,

o impatience; ahent the saft saltire
i trashed, an sheep;
wha's drift on the brae

is a lang cloud's shadda.
the herd cries a wheen wirds
o Tibetan sang,

an A'm waukenet, on a suddenty mindit:
A'm far fae hame,
I hae crossed China.

Xiahe (pronounced *Shi-ah-e*) a Tibetan town in the now Chinese province
of Gansu; **sauch:** willow; **yird:** earth; **slammach:** cobweb.

NOTE

On the journey across China I "met" two historical characters. One was Fa-hsien, a Chinese Buddhist monk of the 4th century A.D. Fa-hsien spent 14 years on the road, travelling through China, Afghanistan and India in his search for holy scriptures. His *Travels* are as fresh today as when he 'wrote down on bamboo tablets and silk an account of what I had been through'. I recognised him in the Buddhist and Taoist wandering monks I saw at truck-stops, fortune-telling to raise a bit of cash, or hitch-hiking, or resting at the doors of yurts.

The other character was equally real. In 640 A.D. the Princess Wen Cheng, plus a considerable entourage, travelled from Beijing to Lhasa as the bride of the king of Tibet. Far from seeking knowledge, she was bringing it with her. R.A. Stein's *Tibetan Civilisation* reads: 'She propagated Buddhism among them [the Tibetans] and built the Rampoche temple at Lhasa. They [the princess and her husband] were given silkworms, brewers, millstones, paper, ink, and glass. The Tibetans still didn't know how to write.'

This pivotal woman entered history and mythology. To this day there is a hill in Amdo province called Sun-Moon Mountain. In a story comparable to that of Eve or Pandora, Princess Wen Cheng broke her 'sun-moon' mirror at this place. The sun-moon symbol, like the yin-yang, is suggestive of harmony and balance.

I began to see ghosts, lines of energy and wanderings, crisscrossed routes of travel. Our own journey was halted at the border of the 'Autonomous Region' of Tibet by the events of the time: general strikes, closed borders, and then on 4th June 1989, the Tiananmen Square massacre.

These poems are my hopelessly inadequate response to those events. They celebrate the journey-makers, the seekers and disseminators of wisdom, those who would declare themselves an 'autonomous region'.

FROM

THE QUEEN OF SHEBA

(1994)

The Queen of Sheba

Scotland, you have invoked her name
just once too often
in your Presbyterian living rooms.
She's heard, yea
even unto heathenish Arabia
your vixen's bark of poverty, come down
the family like a lang neb, a thrawn streak,
a wally dug you never liked
but can't get shot of.

She's had enough. She's come.
Whit, tae this dump? Yes!
She rides first camel
of a swaying caravan
from her desert sands
to the peat and bracken
of the Pentland hills
across the fit-ba pitch
to the thin mirage
of the swings and chute; scattered with glass.

Breathe that steamy musk
on the Curriehill Road, not mutton-shanks
boiled for broth, nor the chlorine stink
of the swimming pool where skinny girls
accuse each other of verrucas.
In her bathhouses women bear
warm pot-bellied terracotta pitchers
on their laughing hips.
All that she desires, whatever she asks
She will make the bottled dreams
of your wee lasses
look like *sweeties*.

Spangles scarcely cover
her gorgeous breasts, hanging gardens
jewels, frankincense; more voluptuous
even than Vi-next-door, whose
high-heeled slippers

keeked from dressing gowns
like little hooves, wee tails
of pink fur stuffed in the cleavage of her toes;
more audacious even than Currie Liz
who led the gala floats
through the Wimpey scheme
in a ruby-red Lotus Elan
before the Boys' Brigade band
and the Brownies' borrowed coal-truck;
hair piled like candy-floss;
who lifted her hands fom the neat wheel
to tinkle her fingers
at her tricks
        among the Masons and the elders and the police.

The cool black skin
of the Bible couldn't hold her,
nor the atlas green
on the kitchen table,
you stuck with thumbs
and split to fruity hemispheres –
yellow Yemen, Red Sea, *Ethiopia*. Stick in
with the homework and you'll be
cliver like yer faither,
but no too cliver,
no *above yersel*.

See her lead those great soft camels
widdershins round the kirk-yaird,
smiling
as she eats
avocados with apostle spoons
she'll teach us how. But first

she wants to strip the willow
she desires the keys
        to the National Library
she is beckoning
    the lasses
      in the awestruck crowd...

Yes, we'd like to
        clap the camels,
to smell the spice,
admire her hairy legs and
bonny wicked smile, we want to take
PhDs in Persian, be vice
to her president: we want
to help her
    ask some Difficult Questions

she's shouting for our wisest man
to test her mettle:

    Scour Scotland for a Solomon!

Sure enough: from the back of the crowd
someone growls:
            whae do you think y'ur?

and a thousand laughing girls and she
draw our hot breath
        and shout:

THE QUEEN OF SHEBA!

Mother-May-I

Mother-May-I
go down the bottom of the lane,
to the yellow-headed piss-the-beds,
and hunker at the may-hedge, skirts
fanned out
      in the dirt and see the dump
where we're not allowed –
twisty trees, the burn, and say:
  all hushed sweetie-breath:
  they are the woods
where men
      lift up your skirt
and take down your pants
even although you're crying.
Mother may I
      leave these lasses' games
        and play at Man-hunt, just
in the scheme Mother
may I
  tell small lies: *we were sot*
in the lane, sat on garage ramps,
picking harling
with bitten nails, as myths
rose thick as swamp mist
from the woods behind the dump
        where hitch-hikers rot
in the curling roots of trees,
and men
leave tight rolled-up
dirty magazines.
Mother may we

      pull our soft backsides
through the jagged may's
white blossom, run across the stinky dump
and muck about
at the woods and burn
        dead pleased
to see the white dye
of our gym-rubbers seep downstream?

A Shoe

On the dry sand of Cramond I found
 a huge
  platform sole, a wedge
of rubber gateau among the o-so
rounded pebbles
  the occasional
washed up san-pro.

I could arrange it in the bathroom
with the pretty
  Queeny shells, God,
we'd laugh, wouldn't we, girls?

  Those bloody bells
ringing down corridors
hauling us this way and that;
 wee sisters and pals
  tugging our hair,
   folders, books
and those shoes – stupid
as a moon walker's; ah,
  the comfort of gravity.

You don't suppose she just
  stepped off the Forth Bridge,
head over heels, shoes self-righting
  like a cat,
hair and arms flying up
 as she slid down through the water?

Or did she walk in, saying yes
  I recognise this
as the water yanked heavy
 on thighs belly breasts?

God girls, we'd laugh:
  it's all right once you're in.
it's all right
  once you're out the other side.

Hand Relief

Whatever happened to friends like Liz,
who curled her legs on a leather settee,
and touched your knee, girl/girl,
as she whispered what the businessmen of Edinburgh
wear beneath their suits –

laughed and hooked her hair back
saying Tuesday, giving some bloke
hand relief, she'd looked up at the ceiling
for the hundredth time that lunch-hour,
and screaming, slammed the other hand down hard
on the panic button; had to stand there
topless in front of the bouncers
and the furious punter, saying
sorry, I'm sorry, it was just a spider...

Whatever happens to girls like Liz
fresh out of school, at noon on a Saturday
waiting for her shift at Hotspots
sauna, in a dressing gown
with a pink printed bunny
who follows you to the window
as you look out at the city
and calls you her pal. She says, *you're a real pal.*

Child with Pillar Box and Bin Bags

But it was the shadowed street-side she chose
while Victor Gold the bookies basked
in conquered sunlight, and though
Dalry Road Licensed Grocer gloried and cast
fascinating shadows she chose
the side dark in the shade of tenements;
that corner where Universal Stores' (closed
for modernisation) blank hoarding blocked
her view as if that process were illegal;
she chose to photograph her baby here,
the corner with the pillar box.
In his buggy, which she swung to face her.
She took four steps back, but
the baby in his buggy rolled toward the kerb.
She crossed the ground in no time
it was fearful as Niagara,
she ran to put the brake on, and returned
to lift the camera, a cheap one.
The tenements of Caledonian Place neither
watched nor looked away, they are friendly buildings.
The traffic ground, the buildings shook, the baby breathed
and maybe gurgled at his mother as she
smiled to make him smile in his picture;
which she took on the kerb in the shadowed corner,
beside the post-box, under tenements, before
the bin-bags hot in the sun that shone
on them, on dogs, on people on the other side
the other side of the street to that she'd chosen,
if she'd chosen or thought it possible to choose.

Fountain

What are we doing when we toss a coin,
just a 5p-piece into the shallow dish
of the fountain in the city-centre
shopping arcade? We look down
the hand-rail of the escalator
through two-three inches of water
at a scatter of coins: round, flat, worthless,
reflections of perspex foliage
and a neon sign – FOUNTAIN.
So we glide from mezzanine to ground,
laden with prams, and bags printed
Athena, Argos, Olympus; thinking: now
in Arcadia est I'll besport myself
at the water's edge with kids,
coffee in a polystyrene cup.
We know it's all false: no artesian well
really leaps through strata
fathoms under *Man at C&A*, but
who these days can thrust her wrists
into a giggling hillside spring
above some ancient city?
So we flick in coins, show the children how:
make a wish! What for, in the shopping mall?
A wee stroke of luck? A something else, a nod
toward a goddess we almost sense
in the verdant plastic? Who says
we can't respond; don't still feel,
as it were, the dowser's twitch
up through the twin handles of the buggy.

Royal Family Doulton

My ladies of the dark oak dresser
I reached for you above the pewter
teapots ribbed like cockles, snaps
taken with the first family Kodak
six months ago when we were wee.

Figurines in mufflers, *Top o' the hill*,
Katherine, ermine, *Demure*'s eyes
lowered in a poke bonnet; I remember
your petticoats, flower baskets,
the delicacy of gloves.

Not my Nana scrubbing floors, her fine mantle
a gas-light's; the shared lavvy, my hand
in her rough fist past the blacked-out
stair-head window no one bothered
to scrape clean, to welcome a dull sun

twenty years since the bombs.
The Doultons' heart-shaped faces
gazed at summer Downs, sparkly ballrooms.
Seized in coy pirouettes, little victims
of enchantment, the tenement was condemned.

Handed down. On the mattresses
of my various floors I saw you trip
along lanes, hold tiny parasols
against the glare of naked bulbs,
peek behind fans in a house

where shaven-haired women
slept in the same bed,
and Jim greased guns for burial
in a revolutionary field.
One day I smothered them

in bubble-wrap, like a mother
I read of who smothered her kids
for fear of the Bomb,
took them back to the safety
of my parents' built-in wardrobe,

in case they got smashed,
little arms and bonnets, parasols
and scattered baskets. One day, I said
I'll have a calm house, a home
suitable for idols; but it hasn't happened yet.

School Reunion

1

We were always the first to get snow
up here in the hills, sagging on roofs
like a shirt tail
        laying on the dreels
rich brown before they built more houses.

It's time. Taxis crunch the gravel
        at the Kestrel Hotel, its fake
coach-lamps shine yellow.
            Come in, we're
                almost
                    all here.

Downstairs, women
who work in banks are dancing, handbags
piled like ashes at their feet.

They raise their arms
in the disco lights, bra straps droop.
those faces turn, eyes, the same
lipstick mouths...
           In the Ladies/
                Girls

A glass vase & twist of plastic fuchsia.
        Laughter   Hairspray
          holds   the air
smiles stale
           fag ash   grey
cubicle doors clang; my shoes are wrong
                the tongue
                shocks with blood
                fuck off you
a pin scratches:

I want McKean
to shag me – Gemma
            is a bitch whore slag tart
                            Our voices
    rise and rise, breasts fall
            toward pink-pastel basins,
                as we take out lipsticks, lean
    into mirrors   look   our mother's faces
                rise to greet us
                framed in paper rosebuds
                from the opposite wall.

2

The child birls in the frosty playground,
her woolly hat, gloves flying on strings.

The text of a dream: wild earth
                            carpet
emulsion in peach blossom.
                Decree Nisi, two years
    South Australia;
                        we have
                        almost all come back

the D.J. who lived down the lane,

Linda   willowy acrobat
divorce   cartwheels, skirts
Expecting   (again)   cover her face

            a mother's grip
    can't you be more
            ladylike,   women
                                beware
                                gravity.

Lorraine Paton   (she's started
Gillian   she's started
that Michelle   She started and all

122

ganging up, the fruity weight of a gang
swaying slowly, ganging up.
                                    You!

          snot-bag
     Ya: Fat boy, Lezzie
ya spaz, gowk, snobby get, ya poofter

that Sandra

we knew each other utterly, the spinning bairn

                    ya lying cow she never
     threw herself under a train

The grey clanging metal lavvy doors.

3
Oh who
            is that: gliding between darkened tables
            turquoise and gold strap, tropical blackhair
            on a bare arm tiny
            diamond in her slender nose o who
                    in the disco-lights...
            Couldn't I have dared to be
            Hazel Thompson, the weight of all hair
            lists her head as though she hears
            birdsong in Africa
            through the stamping disco
            tilts as the diamond
            tugs toward its black mine
            hair grown since we were
            seven   secret as marijuana
            in her dad's shed
                    their council house maroon door.
            I'd like to
            gather up that black hair
            Clarks shoes slapping
            down the street straight and grey
            as a school skirt, rainwater stains
            on harled gables, NO BALL GAMES

to see her in turquoise and gold
give it her in armfuls, Hazel
witchy
sweet as a   *wait, let me*
                        chum you...
Oh who   would have thought it?

4

When we're older than a mattress
on the dump, and shudder
in the living rooms of daughters
who're 60, who put on lipstick and
kindly lead us out
        to lunch in cold hotels
    that smell of paint, specimen
vases with plastic fuchsias
        and our shoes are wrong, shuffling on the red carpet,
    again we'll enter The Kestrel Hotel's
dim loud dance hall;
        as diners turn in the cool light,
mouth open, those appalled young eyes;
    we know whose names we will mutter & shout
                we are almost all here
as our daughters hush us.

5

The first snow. Taxis turn
onto the high road,
the Wimpey scheme's
familiar streets. Distant lights
flash calmly
on the Forth Bridge, warning aircraft.

            The morning after, waking
            in your parents' too-small house,
            the single bed, & wardrobe
            brought from Granny's when she died

                    Today we'll take a walk
                    flat shoes, damp stains
                    on the harled gables;
                    to the fields; perhaps
                    a kestrel
                            hovering still above the road.

Our laughter sealed in taxis, those faces
turn, eyes, same lipstick mouths;
goodbyes   your corner
with the privet hedge whose leaves
like greasy silk you pulled
one by one, under the streetlamp.

                In yellow light, the bairn spins

a coloured twist
within us, like a marble.
                    Close the taxi door and wave
know we are the space
the others ease into
at your old road-end.

The taxi lights recede through the scheme's
dour streets   You watch
            from the same door,
                then let yourself in.

As if
it's never happened
        all that's happened since.

                                                    125

Bairns of Suzie: a hex

Have you not seen us, the Bairns of Suzie
under the pylons of Ormiston Brae
running easy
      with foxes and dogs, high
on the green hill, high
         in the luke-warm mother's glance
  of midwinter sun?

Have you not seen us
        in the rustling whin,
           the black
Gioconda smile of the broom pods?

        Ablow the pine-tree
where a nylon rope
swings from a strong limb?

     Children of Suzie come out to play
on the stone nipple
of the Black Craig

        open-leggèd, chuckling
as Vorlich and Shiehallion
snow-rise across the wide Tay,

   laughing like jackdaws as we peel
      skinny scratches of bramble
        from our inner arms
roll them like cigarettes
between our twig fingers,
         tip them
with jags from the dog-rose
tangled
    in the hair-nests
of each other's armpits and sex:

   fast
   invisible arrows, hexed
         for you

with your laws and guns,
          who'd take this hill,
shake in the people's faces keys
to courtrooms and gates
          the arrows
will enter like stars
find you
staring at the ceiling of your too-hot
          todd-reeking rooms
night after night

until, whey-faced and desperate
you look for culprits
on the dour pavements you'd have us walk
          nose to tail
looking for Bairns of Suzie
among the wifies in scarfs,
the prams at the Co-op door the old boys'
grey-muzzled dogs
by the sunny bench at the mill.

But they will shake their douce heads,
          old seed heads
the keys of larch and rowan berries shaking
and point in different directions
each to their own home,

to the very stones of their homes,
the lintels, thexstanes, hearth
warning that such a red stone
could have come only
from the Abbey and the Grand Castle
ruined utterly
          at the town's edge.

And the Bairns of the witch of this hill
run on, loose limbed & laughing.

Wee Baby

In a dark and private place –
                    your handbag
she knits herself existence.
She sums and divides herself
from half-forgotten phone numbers.

She has slavered on the future
pages of your diary
to make
        a papier-mâché baby
she rubs herself with lipstick,

renders herself visible,
because she only just exists, like a stamp hinge.

She sticks. She dangles from her fathers.
She turns little fishy tricks
in your wine glass: you swallow,
now:
        open your mouth and who cries out?

Wee Baby's come to work:
she is tucked up in the in-tray.
Wee Baby's in the kitchen:
she is cradled in the sieve of all potential.

She blows about the desert in a sand-pram,
O traveller. And driver –
who flashes so indignant
on the outside lane?

She's on the town tonight, she's giving her first smile,
she's playing with her toes
on a high and lonely bar-stool.
You know you're thirty, and she loves you.

The kingdom of Wee Baby is within.
She curls her fists and holds tight.

Wee Wifey

I have a demon and her name is
                WEE WIFEY
I caught her in a demon trap – the household of my skull
I pinched her by her heel throughout her wily transformations
until
     she confessed
                       her name indeed to be WEE WIFEY
and she was out to do me ill.

So I made great gestures like Jehovah: dividing
land from sea, sea from sky,
                       my own self from WEE WIFEY
(*There*, she says, *that's tidy!*)

Now I watch her like a dolly
keep an eye,
        and mourn her:
For she and I are angry/cry
                  because we love each other dearly.
It's sad to note
           that without
                 WEE WIFEY
I shall live long and lonely as a tossing cork.

Outreach

With a stick in the hot dust
I draw a tenement, a plane, a church:
my country we have no
family fields. In a smoke-choked hut
where a barren wife gave birth
they pat the sackcloth, *sit!*
while hens peck round the sleeping kids
and someone coughs, coughs. *What your family?*

Hunkered in the mean shade
of our compound walls: *Your tits
not big!* Our yard grows
nothing, their constant feet.
At noon, the murderous heat,
I clang the gate: *come back tomorrow.*
Perhaps in my heart of hearts
I lack compassion. I lie

hot nights on a straight bed,
watch crowded stars through mosquito mesh
and talk to Jesus. Moonlight
strikes our metal gate like a silent gong.
Sometimes I wake
to a dog's yelp, a screech of owl,
sometimes, a wide-eyed girl
hugely wrapped in shawls. *What your husband?*

I walk a fine line with the headman,
write home: *One day I'll build a church;*
because I believe in these Lazarus' huts
are secret believers;
and listen in village lanes
of bones and dung for Jesus' name
among the shouts, the bleating goats,
the bursts of dirty laughter.

China for Lovers

Darling, we're in China;
a bus station motel. Do you feel
your sweat mix with noodle-steam
and diesel? What place

I can't tell. Our map was nicked
by a sneak-thief in the market square.
Perhaps their need
was desperate. We're at least aware

that we're someplace in China.
So let's quit this rucked grey sheet,
and step into the midsummer midnight heat
of a balcony

that's lost its grip.
As the town clock chimes out
twelve, thirteen, let me whisper:
deep in China means

if something normal
like a telephone's ring
reaches us over the vile latrine,
the barking mongrels, the lost sheep,

the all-night mechanic's metallic beats,
it is not for us. Not once
in the lives of girls asleep
in cauliflower trucks

or their fathers', who in blue serge suits
play cards by gaslight on an upturned box
are our names mentioned.
Now, come back indoors

and take it slow. Who's to know?
Who's to care if a quilt slithers
from a hard bed to a dusty floor,
darling, somewhere in China.

Perfect Day

I am just a woman of the shore
wearing your coat against the snow
that falls on the oyster-catchers' tracks
and on our own; falls
on the still grey waters
of Loch Morar, and on our shoulders
gentle as restraint: a perfect weight
of snow as tree-boughs
and fences bear against a loaded sky:
one flake more, they'd break.

In Praise of Aphrodite
(after Marina Tsvetayeva)

These are wicked days. The very gods,
brought low, fold their wings
like gulls or cushie-doos

white and rain-grey. No honeyed quaich
transforms your sweat;
your low mouth's crowded

where kingdoms flutter,
stoop, take sup from your hands,
your breasts rounded as clouds.

Every flower of the cliff,
saxifrage, thrift, witch-wife:
shows your face. Your body of stone

rising, always rising armless
from the foam, whence we crawl
through salt, sweat, the white spume.

Mr and Mrs Scotland Are Dead

On the civic amenity landfill site,
the coup, the dump beyond the cemetery
and the 30-mile-an-hour sign, her stiff
old ladies' bags, open mouthed, spew
postcards sent from small Scots towns
in 1960: Peebles, Largs, the rock-gardens
of Carnoustie, tinted in the dirt.
Mr and Mrs Scotland, here is the hand you were dealt:
fair but cool, showery but nevertheless,
Jean asks kindly; the lovely scenery;
in careful school-room script –
The Beltane Queen was crowned today.
But Mr and Mrs Scotland are dead.

Couldn't he have burned them? Released
in a grey curl of smoke
this pattern for a cable knit? Or this:
tossed between a toppled fridge
and sweet-stinking anorak: *Dictionary for Mothers*
M:– Milk, *the woman who worries...*;
And here, Mr Scotland's John Bull Puncture Repair Kit;
those days when he knew intimately
the thin roads of his country, hedgerows
hanged with small black brambles' hearts;
and here, for God's sake, his last few joiners' tools,
SCOTLAND, SCOTLAND, stamped on their tired handles.

Do we take them? Before the bulldozer comes
to make more room, to shove aside
his shaving brush, her button tin.
Do we save this toolbox, these old-fashioned views
addressed, after all, to Mr and Mrs Scotland?
Should we reach and take them? And then?
Forget them, till that person enters
our silent house, begins to open
to the light our kitchen drawers,
and performs for us this perfunctory rite:
the sweeping up, the turning out.

Flashing Green Man

I regret the little time I make to consider
these adult days, as you take a photo
to the window, tilt it to the winter light.
Now I'm one of the city. Under the multi's
walking tall and bejewelled
across our dark land, I wait with the others:
thinking about supper and the grocer's wife,
whom he said, as he weighed out potatoes,
had been mugged. But these days I don't much consider.

The green man flashed – he too refuged in cities –
and the traffic stilled for the shouting
news-vendor in his cap and scarf, for us
blethering people; and a sound
in the orange glow: a high *kronk-honk*
that made me picture those ancient contraptions
abandoned on farms. But I stopped
on the rush hour pavement to watch
the skein's arrow
cross the traffic-choked Marketgait,
and head for the glittering multi's
tenth or twelfth floor, where they banked
in the wind of these pivotal buildings
to pull themselves North to the Sidlaws:
and brash light from windows
where clerks tugged on street clothes,
coated their wings in silver and gold;
and people flowed round me
intent on home; from the roundabout's hub
traffic wheeled off to the suburbs.

If not them, perhaps someone high in the multi's –
say a pale-faced woman peeling potatoes
as her husband climbed the long stairs,
listened, smiled, and wiping the window
cupped her hands round her eyes
to acknowledge a sign
truer than the flashing green man

or directional arrows below at a junction
where I watched the geese tilt
to make their turn, their beating wings
more precious than angels' in the city lights.

Arraheids

See thon raws o flint arraheids
in oor gret museums o antiquities
awful grand in Embro –
Dae'ye near'n daur wunner at wur histrie?
Weel then, Bewaur!
The museums of Scotland are wrang.
They urnae arraheids
but a show o grannies' tongues,
the hard tongues o grannies
aa deid an gaun
back to thur peat and burns,
but for thur sherp
chert tongues, that lee
fur generations in the land
like wicked cherms, that lee
aa douce in the glessy cases in the gloom
o oor museums, an
they arenae lettin oan. But if you daur
sorn aboot an fancy
the vanished hunter, the wise deer runnin on;
wheesht ... an you'll hear them,
fur they cannae keep fae muttering
ye arenae here tae wonder,
whae dae ye think ye ur?

Den of the Old Men

C'mon ye auld buggers, one by one
this first spring day, slowly down
the back braes with your walking sticks
and wee brown dugs, saying: *Aye, lass
a snell wind yet but braw.* Ye
half dozen relics of strong men
sat in kitchen chairs
behind the green gingham curtain
of yer den, where a wee dog grins
on last year's calendar – we hear ye
clacking dominoes the afternoon for pennies.
And if some wee tyke
puts a chuckie through the window
ye stuff yesterday's Courier
in the broken pane, saying
jail's too guid fur them, tellies in cells!
We can see your bunnets nod
and jaws move: what're ye up to
now you've your hut built,
now green hame-hammered benches
appear in the parish's secret soft-spots
like old men's spoor?
Is it carties? A tree-hoose?
Or will ye drag up driftwood;
and when she's busy with the bairns
remove your daughters' washing-lines
to lash a raft? Which,
if ye don't all fall out and argue
you can name the *Pride o' Tay* and launch
some bright blue morning on the ebb-tide
and sail away, the lot of yez,
staring straight ahead
                    like captains
as you grow tiny
out on the wide Firth, tiny
as you drift past Ballinbriech, Balmurnie, Flisk
with your raincoats and bunnets,
                    wee dugs and sticks.

Jocky in the Wilderness

Jock, away and tell it to the bees:
they're closing down the factory.
The Post Office women say:
is that old Jock? we thocht he was deid!
If Jocky's deid, who's dossing
in the derelict biggin
at Hazleton Wa's? The slates
are flown, the sternies prick like whin.
Whose pink trampled blanket's this,
whose fist-crushed lager tins?

Jock's a-brawling on the Aberdeen train.
I'll punch your heid! he says to his weans
I'll punch *your* heid! repeat the weans.
The shipyard roof's stripped o lead,
the bosses fled, the plant
is wede awa. At closing time
womenfolk get up and bar the door.
They're shouting through the letterbox:
Jock: enough's enough! awa

and reconstruct yourself
in your various dens; come hame
when ye've learned
to unclench your fists and hert.
So Jock walks the sheuchs
of the parish of his birth
trails of sticky-willy on his poor coat,
scares bairns in the river haar,
in their bedtime tales.
Jock-in-the-ditch are you no feart
they'll concrete over your redundant limbs?
Are you smiling with the foxes yet,
do you ken the wildflowers names?
Den of Milltown, Den of Dens, Den of Lindores.
Jocky's in the wilderness.
Jocky all alane.

One of Us

We are come in a stone boat,
a miracle ship that steers itself
round skerries where guillemots
and shags stand still as graves.
Our sealskin cloaks are clasped
by a fist-sized penannular brooch,
our slippers are feathery
gugas' necks: so delicate
we carried them over the wracky shore,
past several rusted tractors. Truth:
this was a poor place, a
ragged land all worn to holes. No one,
nothing, but a distant
Telecom van, a bungalow
tied with fishing floats
for want of flowers.
                              That August night
the Perseid shower rained
on moor and lily-loch, on a frightened world –
on us, in a roofless shieling
with all our tat: the
golden horn of righteousness,
the justice harp; what folks expect.
We took swans' shape
to cross the Minch, one last fling
with silly magic – at our first
mainland steps a dormobile
slewed into a passing place; cameras flashed.
So we stayed high, surprised
a forester making aeolian flutes
from plastic tubes,
he shared his pay. 'Avoid
the A9. For God's sake,
get some proper clothes.' We ditched
the cloaks, bought yellow
Pringle sweaters in Spean Bridge,
and house by safe house
arrived in Edinburgh. So far so
tedious: we all hold
minor government jobs, lay plans, and bide our time.

Sky-burial

On the litter I tilt, sweat,
sail the day-blue
iris of sky; my eyes
flick open like a doll's.
Friends, am I heavy? You bear me
under larches in their first green,
pink nipply flowers
                    droop, tease my lips.
Iris leaves rustle, babble of streams.
Your feet seek stones, slip
the water's glassy sheen.
Level me, *steady*, your murmurs
could be   turbanned merchants
in far-flung bazaars,
my arms lashed gently to my side.

Are we there? whispers a child, no,
                    the stone trail twists
I out-stare the blind sky,
          twin hawks
spiral the stair of their airy tower,
king & queen calling
repulsed   bound.

A heather plateau;
travelling winds bring home on their backs
scented oils,
          rotting birds, bog-weeds.
Arenas of peat-lips
speak of forests, old wolves.
Dry lochans reveal
                    deer-spoor
creamy long-bones of trees.

Now friends, women in a ring,
raise your arms
part the blue sky

to a dark pupil; intelligent eye,
    ice-black retina of stars

slip me in.

        And if the child asks,
as you dust your hands,
turn down toward home in the green glen

                where do they go, the dead?
              Someone at last
may crack a small joke,

one say she feels watched;
one tug soft arching branches
over the burn.

You may answer him:
        here,   here,

                              here.

Midsummer on the high moor
my eyes flick open:
                  bouquets
of purple iris, midnight
cathedrals of sky.

The wind unravels me
winter birds will arrive.

Sad Bird

A sad bird
has come to the gutter
of the house-next-door, to sit
on the dull metal rim of the rhone.
It's midnight, every other bird
is tidied away. This grey
pigeon or kind of dove hangs
its head, beak on a breast
yellowed in streetlight.
Like an ornament, it softens
the hard line the pitched
slate roof makes with sheer walls,
the house beneath: a derelict
where, daily for a whole year
two workmen, one old, one young,
arrived in a battered car.
The sad bird looks down
on a home now painted cream, pink
around windows
slightly steamed with breath,
looks sadly down
on us, standing hand in hand
on the mild street, quite still.
Perhaps it's
just resting, homing north
feeling the river and north hills,
only resting
the short night. It's we
who whisper 'sad', 'a *sad* bird',
we who feel a small grief, precise
as a drug, measured and dropped
into the bird's plain thought;
like dark that tints
the gloaming above the river
where we've just walked;
– not so much
as to be unbearable, not the dark of
winter. Above us, the bird blinks.

Above it, a silky night
which won't last long, not
too long, still, alone.

The sad bird was there again last night,
on the third night, gone.

Swallows and Swifts

Twitter of swallows and swifts:
'tickets and visas, visas and tickets' –
winter, and cold rain
clears the milky-way of birdshit
where wires cross the lane.

Hagen and the Owls at Glencoe

There's a touch of the witch,
a shaft of God between clouds
a death in the house, and life
is a cobweb of glass.

The cat's buried at the river,
his death weighs like water in a sack
the owls that cry in the night-time
dropped us a mouse with no back.

Such things by the door in the morning!
things to keep you knowing
that God is in the potting shed,
puts your eye to a crack between slats.

The Republic of Fife

Higher than the craw-stepped
gables of our institutes – chess-clubs,
fanciers, reels & Strathspeys –
the old kingdom of lum, with crowns agley.

All birds will be citizens: banners
of starlings; Jacobin crows – also:
Sonny Jim Aitken, Special P.C.
whose red face closed in polis cars

utters *terrible, ridiculous*
at his brother and sister citizens
but we're no feart, not of anyone
with a tartan nameplate screwed to his door.

Citizen also: the tall fellow I watched
lash his yurt to the leafy earth,
who lifted his chin
to my greeting, roared AYE!

as in YES! FOREVER! MYSELF!
The very woods where my friend Isabel
once saw a fairy, blue as a gas flame
dancing on trees. All this

close to the motorway
where a citizen has dangled,
maybe with a friend clutching
his/her ankles to spray

PAY NO POLL TAX on a flyover
near to Abernethy, in whose tea rooms
old Scots kings and bishops in mitres
supped wi a lang spoon. Citizens:

our spires and doocoots
institutes and tinkies' benders,
old Scots kings and dancing fairies
give strength to my house

on whose roof we can balance,
carefully stand and see
clear to the far off mountains,
cities, rigs and gardens,

Europe, Africa, the Forth and Tay bridges,
even dare let go, lift our hands
and wave to the waving citizens
of all those other countries.

The Horse-drawn Sun

We may lie forsaken in the earth's black gut,
but days are still lit, harvests annual,
skies occasionally blue.
So remember. Pay heed.

Our struggle to surface
after thousands of years is, forgive me,
to break up with a nightmare. Apposite
mate for a horse of the light?

Forget it. Were I not sacred
my work would be duller than
turning a threshing mill.
But it's nothing; an honour.

I draw strength from the burden I've hauled
like a Clydesdale through a hundred
closed generations. But what's an age?
a mere night. I sense light

near exhumation, the plough-share
tearing the earth overhead.
– Go on; blind me. Hear the whinny beneath
the tremor of sun underground. Let us out

to raise a new dawn this dull afternoon.
Let us canter high and look down.
This is the sacred horse drawing the sun.
Let's see what they've lost. What they've become.

A Dream of the Dalai Lama on Skye

A summer wind blows the horn of Glen Brittle.
It's a hard walk, Black Cuillin
to his left hand; asks
the midsummer moon
setting over Canna, *what metaphors*
does the market whisper?
If the hills changed shape,
                    who would tell me?
She shines on ditches choked
with yellow iris: butter-lamps
in a temple corner; a snail-shell
in his moonlit palm:
the golden dimple of an icon's smile.
                    He smiles too, notes
the private union of burn and sea,
as one by one, laverocks rise,
irises open. When no one's watching,
he jumps lightly onto Soay
and airborne seeds
of saxifrage, settled
                    on the barren Cuillin
waken into countless tiny stars.

Another Day in Paradise

1

You're running across the sand
of your desert island: something's
arriving. You splash into the sea,
pick it up with both hands. It's a

shoppers-survey-cum-government-demand,
with a slight genetic spelling error:
it's addressed to someone sensible,
someone you might have been...

So: you fold it tenderly
to form a small boat
that flutters in your cupped hands
and wants to sail, but first

you place on board
a sculpture of your own creation:
island totem; an electric blue feather,
a shell, the stretched and cured

pelt of a wild-fruit,
which you wrap around a pebble
in the manner of shepherds
with an orphaned lamb.

The little boat bobs out on a turquoise sea
not to the government,
nor the council
nor the tax-collecters, none of whom can be trusted

but toward the brand shining new
state museum which
on a clear day, glints upright
like a needle just over the horizon.

They will file it in a vault.
It is one of millions. Someone
will dust them. One day
they'll stage an exhibition.

Now it is night. Noises
in the hinterland. Come dawn
you are walking, you have worn
a trench in the sand. Something is lying:

it is: a share offer/a postcard from London
a Barratt home/a ticked box;
a child's whistle blowing itself
with a scented label: Your free gift.

2
You've tied a string of yellow shells
round your ankle there is no one
to say *beautiful* or mutter *silly cow.*
You gave up gazing at the purple sea
turned inland. Didn't you know
whaups flew between palm trees,
coconuts fell to the banks
of peaty lochs with a damp thump?
Didn't you know it could rain here?
Later there became visible
a range of jagged mountains –
it's time to explore.
But because there is no one
you have written on the sand
words you thought you'd forgotten;
        forfauchlet; havers; fowk;
with the rosary of shells round your beautiful ankle
you begin to walk.

3

Following the immense curve of the glacier's spine;
you made up stories to keep yourself whole.
It was once a dragon.
You sang the songs
of your various homelands
in each of their tongues,
to the cold sky. It was easy to imagine,
jumping crevasses, you were the only person alive.
You knew the ice would blind you
like a magic silver shield in a myth.
Till then, you progressed slowly, noting
the remains of insects and birds,
looking for movement on the moraine,
and when you saw it,
knew it for trickery. All the time
you later said, I was listening
for a shepherd or his daughter
to shout from the mountainside
or play a pipe; and I dreamed they'd share
a little hard bread and some cheese,
the bread and cheese, the shout, the pipe,
so real I could smell them on the bright air.

The Sea-house

In this house
are secret rotting wings,
wrecked timbers; the cupboard
under the stair
glimmers with pearl.

The sea-house
rises from dulse; salt winds
boom in its attics. Here:
my tottering
collections of shells, my ballroom
swirling with fulmars.

Morning brings
laundries of wrack,
a sea-maw's grief-shaped wing. Once
a constellation
of five pink buoys.

This place is a stranger's.
Ewers in each high room
hold a little salt water.
My musical box
is a tinkling crab.

The sea-house is purdah:
cormorants' hooked-out wings
screen every chamber. Inside
the shifting place, the
neither-nor

I knock back and forth
like the tongue of a bell
mournfully tolling
in fog, or lie
as if in a small boat
adrift in an upstairs room.

Rooms

Though I love this travelling life and yearn
like ships docked, I long
for rooms to open with my bare hands,
and there discover the wonderful, say
a ship's prow rearing, and a ladder
of rope thrown down.
Though young, I'm weary:
I'm all rooms at present, all doors
fastened against me;
but once admitted start craving
and swell for a fine, listing ocean-going prow
no man in creation can build me.

The Ice Queen of Ararat

My museum of birds' bones, my cold
display of butterflies, my glacier;
you came roped together in a signature
I couldn't read, stare your snowblind eyes
to the shredded clouds, the spire
where wingless creatures huddled, jumped.
The prow swings and blames
the guilty wind, while at your feet
ice-lips part, and speak
of splintered ships' holds, naves.
Curator of my gallery of white and blue,
I say: go on. Test every move with a hard staff.

At Point of Ness

The golf course shifts
uneasily beside the track
where streetlight melts
to a soft frontier with winter dark.
I cross, then, helpless as a ship,
must let night load me, before
moving on between half-sensed
dry-stane walls; day-birds tucked in some nook.
Tonight, the darkness roars.
Even the fishermen's
Nissen hut seems to breathe
beside its spawn of creels,
a dreadful beaching. I walk on,
toward the shore, where night's
split open, the entire
archipelago set as sink-weight
to the sky. A wind's
caught me now; breath frosts,
and I count, to calm me, the Sound's
lighthouses as they shine and fade
across the surge. Graemsay
beams a long systolic five
to one of dark; Hoy a distant
two: two; scattered buoys
blink where skerries drown, then cut
to sea and stars, then
bloom again, weird lilies
wilt and bloom, till,
heart-scared, I have it
understood:
never   *ever*
harm — this,
                    you never could
and run – that constant roar,
the track's black vein; toward salt
lit windows, my own door…

*

Sunshine

gleams the dry-stane dykes'
lovely melanoma of lichen. A wren
flicks on a weathered post
like a dud lighter, by the track
that splits the golf course
from the town's edge to the shore,
where I walk this afternoon
for a breath of air.